Blood, Poo & Dead Skin

The Things Insects Eat

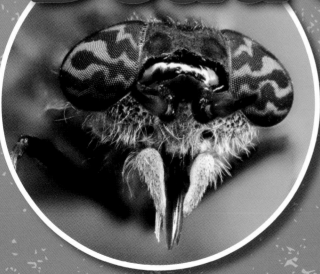

by Ruth Owen and Ross Piper

Published in 2018 by Ruby Tuesday Books Ltd.

Copyright © 2018 Ruby Tuesday Books Ltd.

Editor: Mark J. Sachner
Designer: Emma Randall
Production: John Lingham

Photo credits
Alamy: 14, 21(top), 21 (bottom right); Creative Commons: 15 (top); FLPA: 8, 10, 13 (top), 16, 17 (bottom), 18, 22, 26, 29 (top); Getty Images: 12; Istock Photo: 19; Nature Picture Library: 6, 7, 11, 25; Ross Piper: 5 (centre); Shutterstock: Cover, 1, 4, 5 (top), 5 (bottom), 9, 13 (bottom), 15 (bottom), 17 (top), 21 (bottom left), 24, 27, 28, 29 (bottom left), 29 (bottom right), 31; Gil Wizen: 20.

British Library Cataloguing in Publication Data (CIP) is available for this title.

ISBN 978-1-78856-001-6

Printed in Poland by L&C Printing Group

www.rubytuesdaybooks.com

Words shown in **bold** in the text are explained in the glossary.

Contents

The Things Insects Eat

Crunch, munch, slurp, gotcha! Every second of the day, billions of tiny insects are hunting, **foraging** and eating.

Some insects feed on plants. Others are **predators** that must catch and kill their meals. Many insects are **parasites** that satisfy their hunger by feeding on other living things.

Some **species** of insects are **scavengers**. These mini clean-up crews eat poo or dead bodies. They help dispose of all the yucky stuff that could cause disease or make our world very smelly.

Inside this book, we'll see up-close what happens when some of Earth's tiniest creatures get hungry.

Let's discover what insects eat!

A horsefly

Feeding on Blood

Before she can produce eggs, a female horsefly needs a meal of blood from a large mammal, such as a horse, cow or human. She cuts a hole in her victim's skin with two saw-like **mandibles**. Once blood starts flowing from the wound, she licks it up.

Mandibles

Nature's Dustbins

Cockroaches have a very varied diet. If they live in sewers, they feed on urine, dirty nappies and poo. If they move into your home, they will snack on rubbish, your food, books, plants — even hair and toenail clippings.

A cockroach

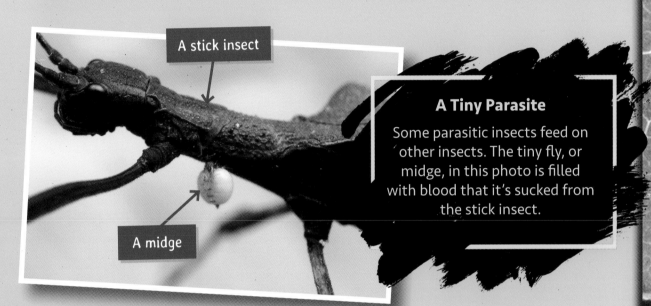

A stick insect

A midge

A Tiny Parasite

Some parasitic insects feed on other insects. The tiny fly, or midge, in this photo is filled with blood that it's sucked from the stick insect.

The Science Stuff–What Is an Insect?

- Insects are tiny animals with a body made of three main parts.

- Insects use their **antennae** to do different things, such as touching, smelling or detecting sounds.

- An insect has a tough outer covering called an **exoskeleton**.

Antennae

The head contains an insect's brain, eyes, mouthparts and a pair of antennae.

The **thorax** has six jointed legs and the insect's wings.

The **abdomen** contains an insect's digestive system and reproductive parts.

Living Larders

Life in a hot, dry desert is tough. So when times are good and there's plenty of food around, it makes sense to store some.

That's exactly what a honeypot ant **colony** does. When desert plants are in bloom, worker ants feed on **nectar** from flowers. They return to the colony's underground nest and feed the nectar to special workers called repletes. The repletes act like living **larders**. Their abdomens grow bigger and bigger as they fill with nectar.

During times when there is no food around, the repletes **regurgitate** the nectar for the whole colony to eat.

Honeypot ants

A honeypot ant's abdomen can swell to the size of a grape!

Too Big To Move

The repletes become so bloated they cannot move. They hang from the ceiling of the nest.

Nectar-filled abdomen

The Science Stuff

When some of the stored nectar is needed, a worker ant strokes a replete's antennae. This signals to the storage ant that it must regurgitate some nectar.

Worker ants also catch and kill other insects, such as wasps. The ants feed on fats from the bodies of their **prey**. Then the fatty liquid is fed to the repletes to be stored for later use.

The honeypot ant in this photo is being kidnapped from its nest by rival ants who want its store of nectar!

Rival ant

Replete ant filled with honey

Honeypot ants live in deserts in Africa, Australia, the United States and Mexico.

Dinner Is Served, Your Majesty!

Butterflies only feed on nectar from flowers, right? Wrong!

Purple emperor butterflies live in the leafy treetops of woodlands in Europe and Asia. These butterflies feed on **sap** that oozes from tree branches. They also feed on a sugary liquid called **honeydew**.

Mmm . . . Sheep droppings.

A male purple emperor butterfly

Oh yes. . . . And sometimes they flutter beautifully down to the ground to suck liquid from a puddle of urine or a pile of animal dung. And if another animal dies in the woodland? You guessed it. The decaying **carcass** is also a great place to find some **nutritious** juices. Dinner is served!

A Royal Insect

A male purple emperor butterfly's wingspan may be more than 7.5 centimetres across. Butterfly fans in the UK have nicknamed this butterfly "Your Majesty".

The Science Stuff

Purple emperor butterflies are rare, and they often don't leave their treetop homes. This makes it difficult for scientists and butterfly fans to see and photograph them.

In July, when the butterflies take flight, people try to lure them down from the trees. They take strange and smelly items into the woods to use as bait.

- Shrimp paste
- Dirty nappies

- Stinky cheese

The strange baits aren't always successful. However, the butterfly fans are thrilled if they get a glimpse of the beautiful insects.

- Dog or fox poo
- Roadkill
- Rotting fish

Disgusting, but Healthy!

Scientists think that purple emperors may not get all the **nutrients** they need from sap or honeydew. The insects may visit animal droppings or dead bodies to get salts.

A female purple emperor butterfly

Proboscis

This female butterfly is sucking up sap from a branch through her **proboscis**.

Fungus Farmers

Deep below the ground in a rainforest, millions of tiny farmers are hard at work. The busy workers are leafcutter ants, and they are growing **fungus** to eat.

To grow their food, the ants need leaves — lots of leaves! Worker ants cut pieces of leaf from trees with their sharp, saw-like mandibles. Then they carry the leaf pieces back to the colony's underground fungus garden.

The leaf material is used to feed the fungus that grows and spreads. Then the ants and their young feed on the fungus.

Mini Minimas

Tiny worker ants called minimas ride on the leaf pieces. They clean any unwanted types of fungi from the leaves. If the wrong type of fungus gets into the nest, it might harm the fungus that the ants are growing.

Minima ant

Worker ant

The Science Stuff

How does fungus farming work?

If you've seen a slice of old bread turn blue and fluffy, you've seen a fungus growing.

That's because the mould on the bread is a type of fungus.

As the mould feeds on the bread, it grows and spreads. That's exactly what happens in an ant colony's fungus garden. The ants get their fungus to grow by feeding it leaves.

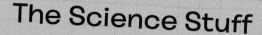

Ants at work in their fungus garden.

Fresh pieces of leaf

Fungus

Meet the Family

Leafcutter ants live in Central and South America. A leafcutter ant nest may be home to more than 15 million ants.

• The queen ant lays up to 30,000 eggs each day. She makes sure there are plenty of new workers to take care of the farm.

• Worker ants collect leaves, take care of the fungus and care for the eggs and **larvae**.

• Soldier ants defend the workers from predators. If an object blocks the workers' path, these much larger ants use their strength to move it.

Munching Moth Caterpillars

If you find holes in your clothes, or bald patches on a rug, this next insect may be sharing your home!

Adult clothes moth

The fibres of a wool jumper

This photo of an adult clothes moth was taken by a powerful Scanning Electron Microscope (SEM). In real life, the moth is just a little bigger than a grain of rice.

A female clothes moth lays up to 200 eggs on clothes, rugs, curtains or even an old teddy bear. She chooses these places because they will give her caterpillars a good supply of food. About 10 days later, tiny, see-through caterpillars hatch and immediately start munching!

A case-bearing clothes moth caterpillar

Case

Case-bearing Clothes Moths

The caterpillars in this photo are the larvae of a case-bearing clothes moth. These caterpillars live inside a case that they make out of fibres from clothes or rugs all stitched together with silk.

The Science Stuff

Clothes moth caterpillars feed on natural materials, such as wool, cotton and fur, that come from living things.

Adult clothes moths don't eat. They live off the food they ate during their caterpillar life stage.

This old teddy bear was made out of real animal fur. Clothes moths have eaten the fur from its face.

The Mini Munchers Grow Up

When they are ready to become adults, the caterpillars spin **cocoons**. Inside their cocoons, they become adult moths. An adult clothes moth lives for less than a month. In that time, it must find a mate and reproduce.

13

Night-time Bloodsuckers

As night falls, tiny bloodsuckers crawl from their hiding places in a bedroom. A bedbug attack is underway!

Bedbugs are insects that feed on human blood. By day, a bedbug hides under a rug, in a wrinkle on a sheet or even behind the wallpaper. At night, it emerges to find a juicy human body.

When it feeds, a bedbug inserts its long, sharp mouthparts into a person's skin. It sucks up blood for about 10 minutes. Then, well fed and double its original size, the tiny bloodsucker goes back into hiding.

Bedbugs on the Hunt

Bedbugs are attracted to carbon dioxide. Humans release this gas as we breathe out.

A bedbug sucking blood from skin

Mouthparts

The Science Stuff

Why do people not wake up when a bedbug bites? A bedbug's saliva contains a substance that numbs the skin.

Normally, human blood clots when the skin is cut. This means the blood gets thick and sticky to help the wounded skin form a scab. Bedbug saliva contains a substance that stops blood clotting. The victim's blood continues to flow until the bedbug has finished its meal.

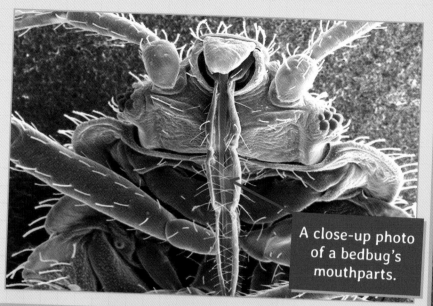

A close-up photo of a bedbug's mouthparts.

Stowaways

Bedbugs can go without food for months and can easily hide in a person's clothes or suitcase. This means the tiny, bloodsucking stowaways can be carried from place to place, and even country to country.

Have You Become a Bedbug Diner?

Here are some ways to tell if bedbugs are dining out in your bed.

- You spot black specks of bedbug poo on your sheets.

- You discover a little reddish-brown smear in your bed. It's possible you've squashed a bedbug that was filled with blood.

- You have red, bumpy, itchy bites on your skin.

- You actually spot a tiny diner arriving to get a meal!

It's Just the Way We Roll

Cow dung, elephant dung — it's all food to a hungry dung beetle.

Fresh dung contains lots of liquid. Adult dung beetles feed on this poo soup as well as eating solid dung.

Some types of dung beetles are known as rollers. The young of these beetles start their lives inside a ball of dung.

A male and female roller dung beetle meet up at a dung pile. Together, they make and bury dung balls. After mating, the female beetle lays her eggs in the dung balls. When larvae hatch from the eggs, they have a ready-made meal of dung waiting for them.

Back off, dung thief!

These roller dung beetles are fighting over dung balls.

There are more than 6000 different species of dung beetles around the world.

Helpful Recyclers

The poo that dung beetles bury in the ground is filled with nutrients that plants need. The dung makes the soil healthier and helps plants grow.

A dung beetle larva eating a dung ball

The Science Stuff

A cow can produce about 36 kilograms of dung in a day. Flies lay eggs in the poo that quickly become more flies. The dung also gets smelly.

When dung beetles bury poo, they keep the land clean and reduce the numbers of flies buzzing around.

Cow dung

A pair of beetles making a dung ball

A Little More Rotting Flesh Anyone?

Blood, poo . . . surely the things insects eat couldn't get any yuckier? Meet the green bottle fly!

Adult green bottles, or blowflies, feed on liquids from rubbish, dung and dead bodies. Their larvae also feed on rotting flesh.

A female green bottle fly lays up to 200 eggs on a decaying body. She lays the eggs in a soft, juicy part of the **corpse**. Once her larvae hatch, they quickly get to work feeding on the dead flesh.

Eaten Alive!

A green bottle may also lay her eggs in a wound on the body of an animal that's still alive. When the larvae hatch, they start feeding on the flesh of their living victim.

Green bottle flies feeding on a dead bird's eye

The Science Stuff

The life cycle of blowflies can be helpful to **forensic scientists** when they investigate a murder. For example, let's say a corpse is discovered in a forest.

Blowflies will visit the dead body soon after death. Scientists can examine the corpse for blowfly eggs, larvae and pupae — the life stage during which a larva becomes an adult.

Scientists know approximately how long each of these life cycle stages usually lasts. Therefore, they can figure out how long the corpse has been in the forest.

CRIME SCENE DO NOT CROSS CRIME SCENE DO NOT CROSS

Rotting flesh

Green bottle fly larvae

For example, if scientists find only eggs, the dead body has probably been in the forest for less than 24 hours. If larvae have already hatched, the body has been in place for several days.

This information could be vital in a murder investigation!

The Insects Strike Back!

Toads feed on insects. So in a battle for survival between an insect and a toad, the tiny insect must be the underdog, right? Not when it's an Epomis beetle larva.

When it's ready to eat, this little insect lures its prey by waving its antennae and hooked mandibles. The movement attracts a toad that thinks it's about to catch a snack. As the toad tries to grab the larva, the insect launches a counterattack.

Leaping onto the toad, the larva sinks its mandibles into its victim. Now, the toad is doomed and will slowly be eaten alive!

Toad

Epomis beetle larvae only feed on amphibians, such as frogs and toads.

An Epomis beetle larva

Hooked mandibles

Epomis beetle larva

A Parasitoid

An Epomis beetle larva is a type of parasitoid. This means it feeds on a living animal and eventually kills that animal.

The Science Stuff

A toad might manage to grab the larva with its tongue before the insect strikes. But the bigger animal is still in trouble. The larva will latch onto its attacker's tongue and start feeding.

If the larva is swallowed, it attaches to the toad's throat or stomach. Then it begins its meal from inside its prey!

An adult Epomis beetle

Toad

Some of My Favourite Things . . .

When an Epomis beetle larva becomes an adult, it feeds on other insects and spiders. If it spots a frog or toad, however, it pounces, and digs in to its favourite food from when it was young.

A Dead Bug Backpack

In ancient times, warriors displayed the heads of their enemies on spikes. They might even show off the dead bodies of their slaughtered opponents after a battle.

Big eyes for spotting prey

Heap of ant corpses

Assassin bug

What's all this got to do with insects and their food? Welcome to the world of the **assassin** bug.

There are thousands of different species of assassin bugs. Some, however, feed on their prey and then carry the corpses of their victims around on their backs!

The Science Stuff

An assassin bug has beak-like mouthparts that can stab like a dagger and suck like a straw.

The bug stabs its prey through the exoskeleton with its mouthparts. Then it injects substances into its victim to kill it and turn its insides to liquid. Next, the bug slurps up its prey's liquefied body.

Finally, the assassin bug puts the dry, empty shell of its victim onto its back.

Why Carry Corpses on Your Back?

Scientists think the gruesome backpack of tiny corpses may help the bug in three ways.

First, it helps disguise the bug. This makes it more difficult for predators to know what on Earth they are looking at.

Assassin bugs hunt for small insects such as ants, termites and bees.

Second, the smell of the ant corpses disguises the assassin bug's smell. Third, if a predator takes a bite, it may only get a mouthful of dead ants — not the assassin bug.

A Flower with Bite!

This next tricky predator looks like a beautiful flower, but in fact it's a deadly hunter.

For many years, scientists believed the orchid mantis looks like a flower so it can stay hidden from its prey. Today, scientists think the mantis actually wants flies, bees and other insects to see it.

The mantis's body is shaped and coloured a little like a flower to attract prey. When a fly buzzes by, it doesn't notice the mantis's big eyes or legs. All the fly sees is a pink and white flower that will be filled with delicious nectar. The fly zooms in to pick up a meal, and — gotcha!

A mantis has two large, spiked front legs for grabbing and holding prey.

Front legs

An orchid mantis

How Big Is an Orchid Mantis?

An adult female orchid mantis is about 6 centimetres long. An adult male is much smaller at just 2.5 centimetres long.

The upper sections of an orchid mantis's four walking legs are shaped to look like petals.

A mantis on an orchid

Petal-shaped legs

The Science Stuff

When an animal looks like something else, it's called mimicry. Many insects mimic something such as a leaf or twig to hide from predators. The orchid mantis mimics a flower in order to attract its prey. This is called aggressive mimicry.

A Big Meal for Baby

When it comes to feeding her larva, only one food is good enough for a mother tarantula hawk wasp — a huge tarantula!

A female tarantula hawk goes head to head with a tarantula.

A tarantula

After she's mated, a female tarantula hawk hunts for a tarantula. Often the spider is much bigger than the wasp. Avoiding the spider's deadly fangs, the wasp chooses her moment, and attacks. She flips the tarantula over and stings it. The tarantula is instantly **paralyzed**.

A tarantula hawk wasp

The wasp drags the paralyzed tarantula into a burrow she dug earlier. Sometimes, she imprisons a spider in its own burrow. Then the wasp lays an egg on the tarantula, seals up the burrow's entrance, and leaves.

When a larva hatches from the egg, it eats the paralyzed tarantula — alive!

Fresh and Juicy

A tarantula hawk larva carefully eats the least important parts of the tarantula's body first. This helps keep the larva's meal alive and fresh for days.

An adult wasp feeding on nectar

The Science Stuff

Adult tarantula hawks feed on nectar from flowers.

Male tarantula hawks don't help with feeding or raising their young. Males have no stingers as they don't need to sting and capture tarantulas.

27

Terror Beneath the Sand

An antlion larva doesn't just hunt. This insect sets a trap for its prey, and then it waits to make its kill!

An antlion starts life as an egg buried in sandy soil. Once the hungry larva hatches, it prepares its trap by digging a pit. Then it buries itself at the bottom of the pit, and waits.

Soon, an ant comes scurrying by and falls into the pit. Before the ant can escape, the antlion larva's huge snapping jaws emerge from underground and drag the ant to its death.

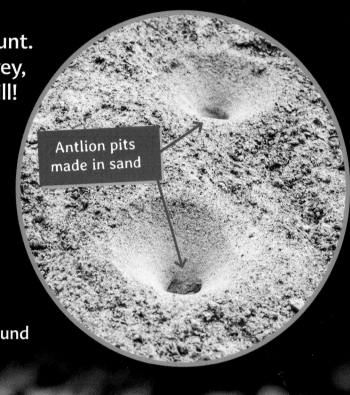

Antlion pits made in sand

Deadly jaws

An antlion larva

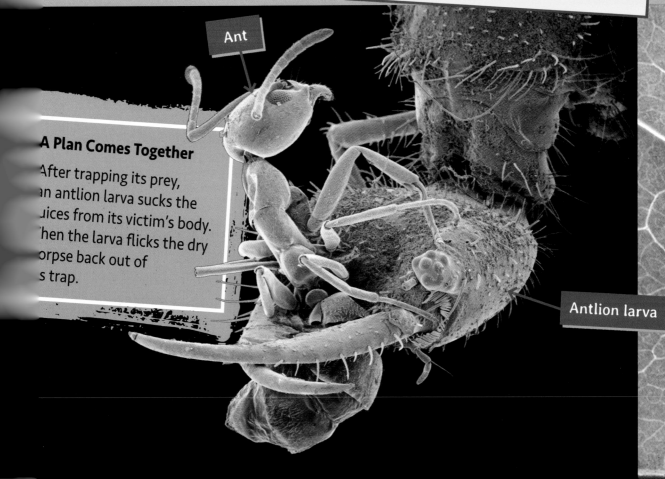

Ant

Antlion larva

A Plan Comes Together

After trapping its prey, an antlion larva sucks the juices from its victim's body. Then the larva flicks the dry corpse back out of its trap.

The Science Stuff

An antlion may live as a larva for up to three years.

An antlion larva

Then the larva makes a cocoon of sand and silk that it spins from its bottom. Inside the cocoon, it becomes an adult.

An adult antlion

Adult antlions can fly. They feed on nectar, pollen and small insects.

29

GLOSSARY

abdomen
The rear section of an insect's body that contains its digestive system and reproductive organs.

antennae
Two long, thin body parts on the head of an insect that it uses for gathering information about its environment.

assassin
A killer.

carcass
A dead body.

cocoon
A protective case made by some insect larvae. A larva pupates inside its cocoon.

colony
A large group of insects that live together and work together to find food, raise young and protect each other.

corpse
Another word for a dead body.

exoskeleton
The hard covering that protects the body of an insect.

forage
To look for and gather food.

forensic scientist
A scientist who examines evidence found at a crime scene.

fungus
A living thing from a group that includes mushrooms, toadstools and moulds.

honeydew
A sugary substance produced by some insects, such as aphids. Honeydew is a waste product that aphids release from their bottoms.

larder
A cupboard or room where food is stored.

larva
The young form of some animals, including insects, fish and frogs.

mandibles
Insect mouthparts that are used for grabbing, cutting, crushing or sucking.

nectar
A sugary liquid produced by flowers.

nutrients
Substances such as vitamins or minerals that living things need to grow and be healthy.

nutritious
Containing nutrients.

paralyze
To make unable to move.

parasite
A living thing that spends part or all of its life living and feeding on another living thing.

predator
An animal that hunts and eats other animals.

prey
An animal that is hunted by other animals for food.

proboscis
Insect mouthparts used for sucking up liquids.

regurgitate
To vomit up something that has been swallowed.

sap
Liquid inside a plant made up of water and nutrients.

scavenger
An animal that feeds on dead plants, carcasses or garbage.

species
Different types of living things. The members of an animal species look alike and can produce young together.

thorax
The middle part of an insect's body between its head and abdomen. The thorax has six jointed legs and an insect's wings.

Millions of Insects

Scientists have identified about one million different insect species. There are millions more yet to be discovered, identified and studied.

INDEX

LEARN MORE ONLINE

To learn more about what insects eat, go to:
www.rubytuesdaybooks.com/insects